IF YOU WERE A KID AT
The First
Thanksgiving

BY MELISSA SARNO • ILLUSTRATED BY LLUÍS FARRÉ

CHILDREN'S PRESS®
An Imprint of Scholastic Inc.

Content Consultant
James Marten, PhD, Professor and Chair, History Department, Marquette University, Milwaukee, Wisconsin

NOTE TO THE READER, PARENT, LIBRARIAN, AND TEACHER: This book combines a historical fiction narrative with nonfiction fact boxes. While all the nonfiction fact boxes are historically accurate and true, the fiction comes solely from the imaginations of the author and illustrator.

Photos ©: 9: Joseph Sohm/age fotostock; 11: David C. Brewster/Wikimedia; 13: NativeStock/North Wind Picture Archives; 15: Fly/Dreamstime; 17: Gabbro/Alamy Images; 19: Head of Squanto (wood), American School, (17th century)/Private Collection/Bridgeman Art Library; 21: DON TREADWELL/iStockphoto; 23: SSPL/Getty Images; 25 left: Metta image/Alamy Images; 25 right: Floortje/iStockphoto; 27: Brady National Photographic Art Gallery/Library of Congress.

Library of Congress Cataloging-in-Publication Data
Names: Sarno, Melissa, author. | Farre, Lluis, 1970– illustrator.
Title: If you were a kid at the first Thanksgiving / by Melissa Sarno ; illustrated by Lluis Farre.
Description: New York : Children's Press, an Imprint of Scholastic Inc., 2017. | Series: If You Were a Kid | Includes bibliographical references   and index.
Identifiers: LCCN 2016038595| ISBN 9780531223833 (library binding) | ISBN 9780531230978 (paperback)
Subjects: LCSH: Thanksgiving Day—History—Juvenile literature. | Plymouth (Mass.)—History—Juvenile literature.
Classification: LCC GT4975 .S37 2017 | DDC 394.2649—dc23
LC record available at https://lccn.loc.gov/2016038595

All rights reserved. Published in 2017 by Children's Press, an imprint of Scholastic Inc.
Printed in the United States of America 113
SCHOLASTIC, CHILDREN'S PRESS, and associated logos are trademarks and/or registered trademarks of Scholastic Inc.
1 2 3 4 5 6 7 8 9 10 R 26 25 24 23 22 21 20 19 18 17

TABLE OF CONTENTS

A Different Way of Life

In 1620 a group of settlers sailed from England to America to find a better life. They sailed on a ship called the *Mayflower* and made their home in what would become Plymouth, Massachusetts. At the time, this area was also home to a group of Native Americans known as the Wampanoag. Imagine you were a kid during the first Thanksgiving, also known as the harvest celebration of 1621. Whether you were a Native American or an English settler, you would have spent much of your time growing or hunting for food. To celebrate the year's successful farming, you might have set aside several days to eat, play games, and give thanks for what you had.

Turn the page to visit this amazing time in American history! You will see that life today is a lot different than it was in the past.

Meet Miles!

Miles Allterton is an English settler who lives in Plymouth **Colony** with his parents. Miles is a friendly boy. He misses his life in England, where he lived before moving to America a year ago. There, he had lots of friends and lived in a big, bustling city. He treasures a handmade necklace which he keeps to remember his favorite aunt, who died on the trip from England to America. . . .

Meet Aquina!

Aquina is a Native American girl who lives in what is now known as Massachusetts. Aquina is very spirited. She loves nature and the outdoors. She wishes she could go on hunting trips with her two brothers and father. But in her family, girls are expected to stay behind to cook and grow food. . . .

It was a chilly evening in November when Miles sat down for dinner with his parents in their home in Plymouth Colony.

"I have an important chore for you tomorrow," said Miles's father. "The colony needs your help."

An important chore? Miles wondered what it could be.

A TROUBLED JOURNEY

The *Mayflower* set sail from England on September 6, 1620, with 102 passengers and two dogs. The trip to America was not easy. There were many storms, and people got seasick. Some even died. The ship was supposed to land at the mouth of the Hudson River in present-day New York, but it landed in Massachusetts instead. The settlers set up Plymouth Colony where they landed.

The *Mayflower*

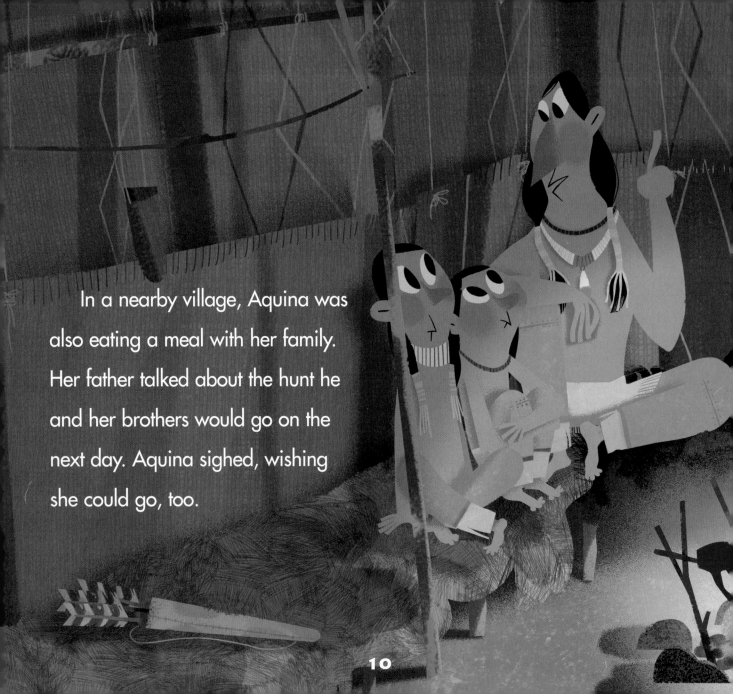

In a nearby village, Aquina was also eating a meal with her family. Her father talked about the hunt he and her brothers would go on the next day. Aquina sighed, wishing she could go, too.

TENSIONS

The Wampanoag and the English settlers had trouble trusting each other. They didn't understand each other's customs and beliefs. A Native American man named Samoset was the first to welcome the English settlers to their land. A few days later, the Wampanoag leader Massasoit signed a peace **treaty** with the English settlers. For many years, the Wampanoag and the English tried to get along. But in 1662, war broke out between them.

A statue of Massasoit

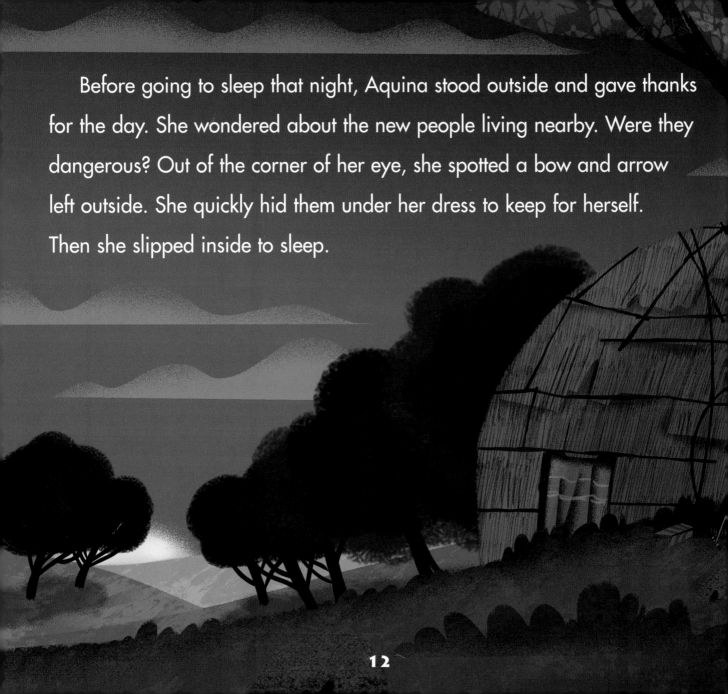

Before going to sleep that night, Aquina stood outside and gave thanks for the day. She wondered about the new people living nearby. Were they dangerous? Out of the corner of her eye, she spotted a bow and arrow left outside. She quickly hid them under her dress to keep for herself. Then she slipped inside to sleep.

A CIRCULAR HOME

Wampanoag families lived in huts called *wetus*. A wetu was made of woven grass or bark. Inside were woven mats for sleeping and a fire pit for cooking.

The Wampanoag were semi-**nomadic**. In warm weather, they lived in open areas where they could grow crops. In cold weather, they moved to wooded areas to stay warm.

A wetu

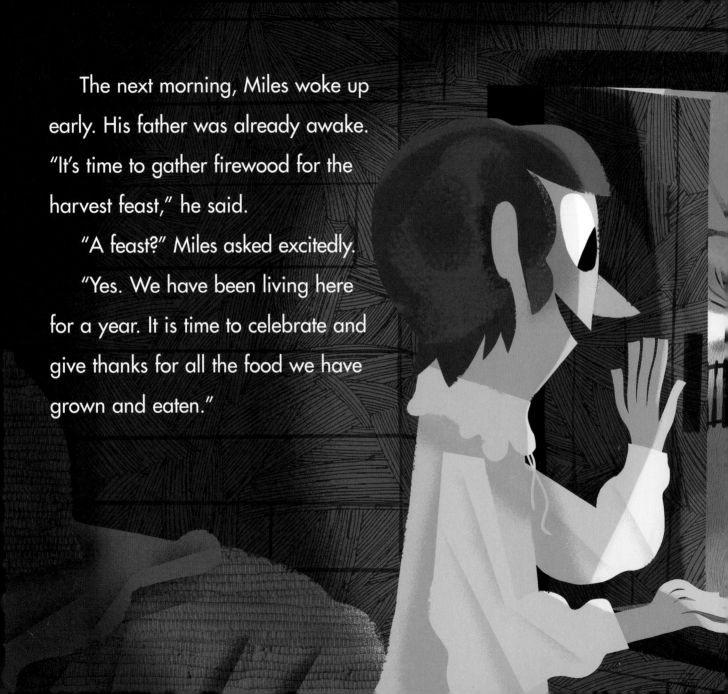

The next morning, Miles woke up early. His father was already awake. "It's time to gather firewood for the harvest feast," he said.

"A feast?" Miles asked excitedly.

"Yes. We have been living here for a year. It is time to celebrate and give thanks for all the food we have grown and eaten."

WATER AND WOOD

Today, you get your water from the sink. Your house is probably heated using gas or electricity. If you were a Wampanoag or an English settler, you would have to collect water from a nearby water source in buckets that were sometimes very heavy. You would also collect a lot of firewood to use to cook your food and to stay warm.

A wooden bucket for collecting water

Aquina woke up to hear her father and brothers leaving for the hunt. Feeling the bow and arrow beneath her blanket, she wondered if she should follow. Watching her mother sleep peacefully, she decided that she would never have such a good chance. She quickly grabbed supplies and snuck off into the woods behind her family.

ON THE HUNT

Today you can buy your food at the grocery store. But Native Americans and early European settlers had to grow their own food or go hunting. The Wampanoag used bows and arrows to hunt deer and spears to fish. English settlers used guns to hunt ducks and other animals. They also walked the shore to collect shellfish.

People carried arrows in a container called a quiver.

After working hard all morning gathering wood, Miles sat down on a tree stump to rest. Suddenly, he heard a loud snapping sound. He turned to see a girl slip and fall in the woods. He ran to her and offered his hand to help.

"Hello," he said.

Aquina shook her head. She did not speak English.

"Miles," he said, pointing to his chest.

"Aquina," the girl said with a smile.

SHARING NEW LANGUAGES

The settlers and the Wampanoag spoke different languages. However, some Wampanoag knew English. A Wampanoag man named Squanto served as an **interpreter** between the settlers and the Wampanoag chief. Many other Wampanoag continued to learn to speak English. However, most settlers did not learn the Wampanoag language.

A sculpture of Squanto

In the distance, Aquina's brothers and father watched Miles and Aquina. Was this boy trying to hurt her?

Just then, they all heard shots being fired. Aquina was frightened by the noise. She grabbed her bow and arrow and ran deeper into the woods to her family. Miles sighed. He thought he had made a new friend, but now she was gone. He touched his aunt's necklace in his pocket. It always made him feel better.

DRESSING UP

The English settlers and the Wampanoag had to make their own clothes by hand. If you were a Wampanoag, you would wear very little. Boys wore a **loincloth**. Sometimes they also wore leggings and a shirt. Girls wore similar clothes. Sometimes they added a skirt. Both wore **moccasins** on their feet. If you were a settler, you would wear layers of clothing. Girls wore a **petticoat**. Boys wore stockings and pants.

Native Americans sometimes used beads to decorate moccasins.

Later that evening, Aquina's father scolded her for following along. Then he explained the loud noises they had heard. It was simply the English firing guns as they hunted. They were planning a feast, and they had invited Aquina's family to join.

A DIFFERENT KIND OF SCHOOL

Learning was very different for the Wampanoags and the English settlers. If you were a Wampanoag, most of your learning was done outside. You would learn how to hunt, cook, and make useful items. If you were English, your parents might teach you to read and write. Religion would be the main subject you studied.

A book about plant life from the 1600s

The next day, the feast began. Everyone gave thanks, played games, and ate delicious food. Miles was surprised to see that a group of people dressed like Aquina were also there. "We invited our neighbors," Miles's father told him. It was then he saw Aquina with her family. He ran over to her to say hi.

A MODERN THANKSGIVING

When we celebrate Thanksgiving today, we watch parades and football on television. It is tradition to eat turkey and pumpkin pie. But during this first Thanksgiving, people were more likely to eat corn, duck, mussels, and deer meat. And while we celebrate Thanksgiving for just one day, the first feast lasted for three days straight.

Many kinds of food were served at the first Thanksgiving.

25

Aquina looked at Miles with suspicion. Miles wondered how he could show her that he wanted to be friends. He pulled his aunt's necklace from his pocket and offered it to Aquina. Aquina put it on and smiled proudly. Later on, she took Miles's hand to show him a traditional game. They were both excited to have a new friend!

A NATIONAL HOLIDAY

Although the first harvest celebration was in 1621, Thanksgiving did not become an official holiday until 1863. President Abraham Lincoln declared a day in November to give thanks for "general blessings." This became the Thanksgiving holiday we celebrate today.

President Abraham Lincoln

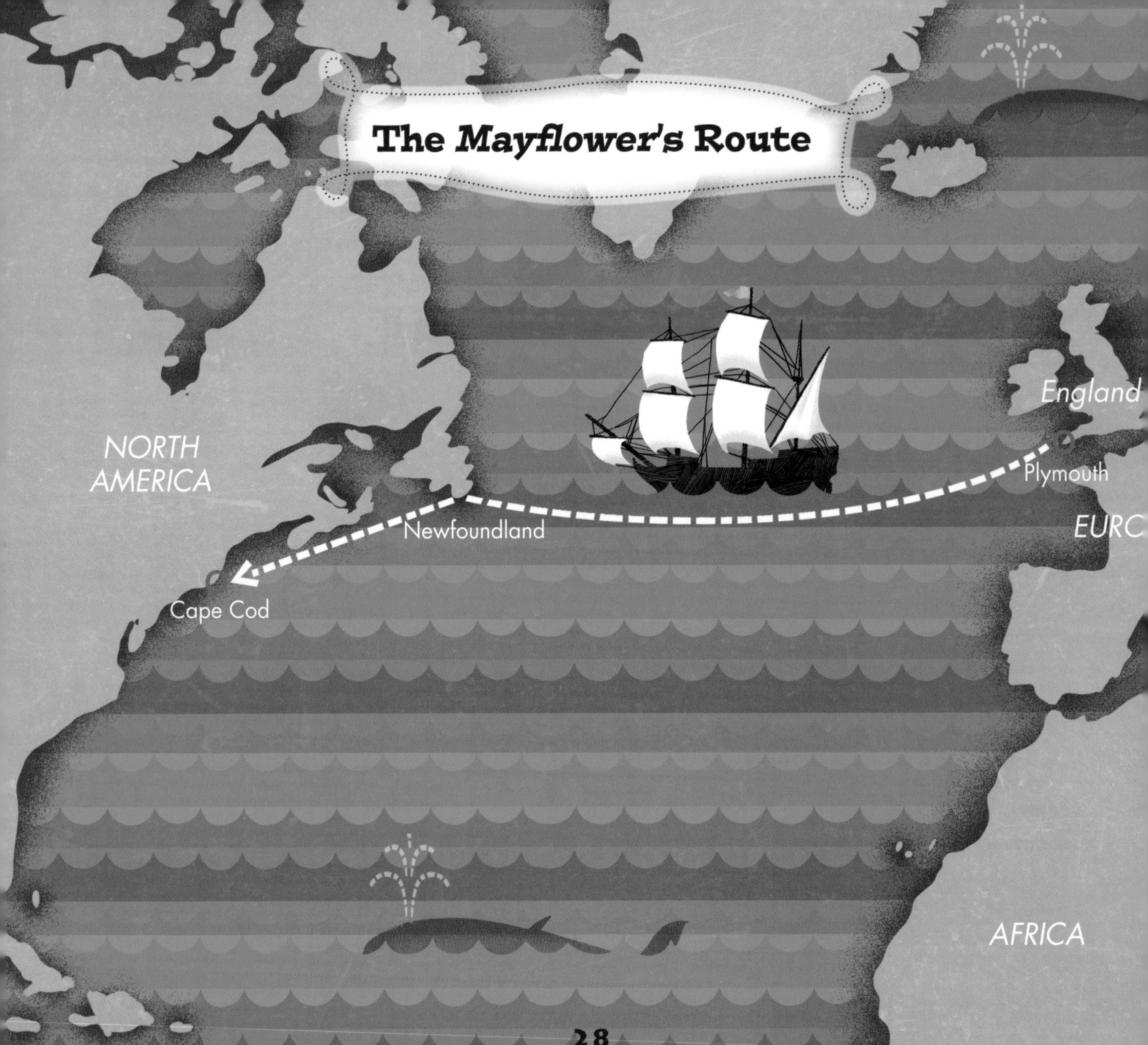

The *Mayflower's* Route

NORTH
AMERICA

England

Plymouth

EURO

Newfoundland

Cape Cod

AFRICA

Timeline

September 6, 1620 The *Mayflower* leaves Plymouth Harbor in England.

November 9, 1620 The *Mayflower* lands in Cape Cod, Massachusetts.

December 1620 The English settlers establish Plymouth Colony.

March 1621 A Native American man named Samoset introduces himself to the settlers in Plymouth Colony. A few days later, the English settlers sign a peace treaty with the Wampanoag leader Massasoit.

Autumn 1621 The English settlers hold a harvest celebration and invite the Wampanoag.

October 3, 1863 President Abraham Lincoln declares that the last Thursday in November will be celebrated as a day of Thanksgiving.

Words to Know

colony (KAH-luh-nee) a territory that has been settled by people from another country and is controlled by that country

interpreter (in-TUR-prih-tur) someone who translates a conversation between people who speak different languages

loincloth (LOIN-klawth) a piece of cloth worn wrapped around the hips

moccasins (MAH-kuh-sinz) flat, soft leather shoes or slippers

nomadic (noh-MAD-ik) belonging to a community that travels from place to place instead of living in the same place all the time

petticoat (PET-ee-kote) a light, loose undergarment that hangs from the shoulders or the waist and is worn underneath a dress or skirt

treaty (TREE-tee) a formal written agreement between two or more countries

Index

ABOUT THE AUTHOR

Melissa Sarno is a writer living in Brooklyn, New York. She writes the content for many best-selling interactive toys, books, and games for kids.

Visit this Scholastic Web site for more information about the First Thanksgiving:

www.factsfornow.scholastic.com

Enter the keywords **First Thanksgiving**

ABOUT THE ILLUSTRATOR

After illustrating more than 100 books over the past 20 years, Lluís Farré has drawn about 40 witches, 200 dragons, 500 princesses (and the corresponding princes), and more than 1,000 kids from different parts of the world and different moments in history. He lives in the coastal city of Barcelona, Spain.